The Floor Keeps Turning

Winner of the United States Award
of the International Poetry Forum
1969

THE FLOOR KEEPS TURNING

Poems *by*
Shirley Kaufman

University of Pittsburgh Press

Some of the poems in this volume have appeared in the *Atlantic Monthly, Burning Bush, Choice, Doors & Windows, Guabi, Harper's, Kayak, The Nation, New American Review, Poetry, Poetry Northwest, Quarterly Review of Literature, Shenandoah, Southern Review,* and *Synapse.*

The poem "Beetle on the Shasta Daylight" originally appeared in *The New Yorker,* "For a Cold Night" in *Poetry.*

Some of the poems also appear in *Quickly Aging Here—Some Poets of the 1970s* published by Doubleday/Anchor Books.

The William Carlos Williams quotation is from "The Descent" in *Pictures from Brueghel and Other Poems,* copyright 1948 by William Carlos Williams, reprinted by permission of New Directions Publishing Corp.; the Rainer Maria Rilke quotation is from "First Elegy" in *The Duino Elegies,* W. W. Norton, 1939; the George Seferis quotation is from *Collected Poems, 1924–1955,* Princeton University Press, 1967.

The International Poetry Forum
and the University of Pittsburgh Press
acknowledge with gratitude the assistance
of the Junior League of Pittsburgh, Inc.,
in making this book possible.

For
Bernie
Sharon, Joan and Debbie

Contents

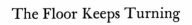

The Floor Keeps Turning

I

A

world lost,

  a world unsuspected

    beckons to new places

and no whiteness (lost) is so white as the memory

of whiteness   .

William Carlos Williams

His Wife

But it was right that she
looked back. Not to be
curious, some lumpy
reaching of the mind
that turns all shapes to pillars.
But to be only who she was
apart from them, the place
exploding, and herself
defined. Seeing them melt
to slag heaps and the flames
slide into their mouths.
Testing her own lips then,
the coolness, till
she could taste the salt.

Turtles

Natives of Chagos
strip the shell
from living turtles.

They buck through
the delicate coral,
where men ride them
down to tie them,
heaping their backs
with fire.
          Travelers
have seen the bony
back
   crack upward,
flames climbing
the curling shell.

Knives force it
from them. Living,
they go on living,
soft, gelatinous
bodies like sinking
rafts.
     They weep
in the water, bury
their sad eyes. Return
in a new shell
thin as an old man's
skin.
     Grieve more
than a hundred
years,
     die usually
from accidents.

Casualties

Mornings I toast the bread
still frozen, reading the news.
Always it burns. The dead
stare out of their numbers
every day. I sit under

the table where it's safe
and peel my orange. The air
smells like the night before.
I keep the windows closed
against the cold.

Strangers are painting
their faces in the front yard.
They run thick fingers
over their feathers,
making them smooth.

My daughter passes
the jam in a silver jar.
She calls to the Indians
a language like fountains
I don't understand.

They sift beads
through their toes,
amber and turquoise,
refracting the light
on strings of rain.

Under the table
I recite the names
of my ancestors.
I have nothing
to go with the jam.

5

The Hunger

And the hunger
coils out of its cave
in the center,
sprouts out of the ribs
like fireworks,
comes grinding,
hunger to hunger,
the back of the eye alive
with two melons
under a vine.

The hunger travels
an old horizon
to a dangerous feast
not yet prepared,
to a banquet
where someone is
sweeping crumbs
from the table
too soon,
to the fruit
false as children
who never came back,

while the melons suck
their own juices
under the rind.
The little pale kernels
shake
    in their dark
        dome.

"Je Suis Belle"

1

I am that animal I started from.
My bones lengthen,
grow silently to their own causes.
Even my ankles seem dangerous,
skin of my instep stretching
over the arch.
My arms are wrapped in thick fur;
carnivorous birds fly out of my wrists
when we begin to stroke the air.

2

Safer than rooms,
whatever hollow in the earth
I made, small-breasted as a child,
and knew by other faces
in the dark. Now graffiti
on the walls glitter
like an old family; those ancient
bulls keep watch.
Amber and ochre, color
of winter pears. They glow,
purely the cave's invention,
and we move in them reflected,
reach for unchanging signs
and give off light.

3

You bring me distance, warm
vineyards sloping to Lac Léman,
evenly terraced as your breathing evenly
without dreams. That castle in Lausanne.
The queen of Spain slept there, they said,
as if a throne climbed into bed

with castanets. Dark oak
and deeply carved. The skin of a queen
must be softer than tongues
when she leans against great pillows.
Rainwater, when you drown
your fingers in it. Deep.

4

"Je suis belle" . . . as a sleep of stone:
you seek that part of me
I would not lose,
just as those Rodin hands
in their tense bronze sob
in the flesh of her giving
and withholding. She bends
and folds over, exceeding herself.
And he lifts her, lifts her,
clutches her smoothness, thrusts
his chin into the moss of her neck.

5

The night is alive with shadows,
ships scraping up to the docks,
waves slapping around the wood,
bulkheads creaking, queens sailing
into a storm, cinders
of spray—such motion in the wind
that everything gives way—anchor
and line, shape of that wrinkled harbor,
and we rock, we rock,
we rock and we are visible
each to the other as nothing
was ever visible before.

Brides

He fathered twelve, my grandfather,
and when he walked in his rose garden,
leaves splashing and the fire
of uncut blooms, sunlight
on his skullcap's silk like sparks,
the Sisters came and went
in black next door.

One day I asked him why
they wore gold wedding rings.
He gathered the shape of my shoulder
in his hand. "They married
the church," he smiled
out of his opulent beard.
Grown older

and the nights warm with parables,
I lay my body on its bed
stretched to its own feeling,
wondering what he meant,
while brides in black
danced on my
grandfather's ceiling.

Behind Me

Why does he follow
silent all the way
to my old house

never asking why
I am still poking in corners
kicking over the shards
worm-glitter
pelts
out of my sleep blinking
waking into a swarm
of tricks and morning
flying between the roofs
like Monday wash

I won't turn around
to measure my distance from him
wanting to understand it
all at once
(and without training)

light on the waters
radiance turned to fire
the fire a throne
then angels
                blazing
wings
or ways more sudden

he doesn't even sigh
but all the same I know
if I just turn
my head he'll be there

flapping the prayer shawl
like a gull spread sideways
he'll haul his own
brutality of faith
or seizure

all the way
he never takes my arm
to stop me saying you
can't go back
or why do you still
look for the place
or what makes you think
that it was ever
there

Beetle on the Shasta Daylight

for Reggie Kriss

Hills moved. I watched their shadows
riding by like names said
only once. The oaks turned round
and leaves ran past my head.

It was all reeling back where
the old disasters hung between
locked doors stitching the air,
unheard, as if they'd never been.

And the sun came falling through
the window of the train; it filled
my lap, slid down my arms into
the aisle, a blazing river spilled

inside. I found her in the shallow
light, wearing her skeleton
strapped smooth over her belly,
wallowing on her back, alone.

Some little Pequod spitting, mastheads
tufted with joints like unfleshed frogs,
lame as a butterfly spread
on a pin. And from the thrashing legs

hooks caught at nothing, casting
and casting in the air, her
bent and beaded feelers lashing
until the threads would have to tear.

Pharaohs watched her push her dung ball
on the sand the way the sun
rolled slowly over heaven, saw
how she hatched her children

out of that roundness, called her Life.
They made her image out of stone,
greener than stems, to celebrate
the ornamental lake a queen

had built, to mark a lion hunt
or even marriage. They sent
her gleaming in the tombs of all
the dead so they might rise again.

I didn't touch her; slipping a marker
from my book under her back,
I turned my wrist down gently, set her
right. A piece of the whole shook

world turned up. Alive! She was
amazed to flex herself, to feel
the sun along her side like juice,
to have her front legs wheel

her forward, arched in a priestly
benediction. Oh she was tight. She served
her concentrated self, and neatly.
Her eyes glittered out of her head.

Lightly she went and steady down
the aisle. Not any landscape she
remembered. Yet she was sure of home,
composed her dark wherever she might be

creeping. I waved her well. Saw
that she left no furrow in the floor.
But someone got up, swelling out
of his seat and raised his foot, before

13

my hand could drop, and put it down
and passed into the next car
and was gone. There was no sound
but the train's sound. Far

down the tracks, the sun rolled over.
I had to sit there after that
and look at California moving
backward, pressing my face flat

against the glass until it froze
to my skin. All afternoon
I looked out at the hills, those
trees with the light crawling down

their branches like white beetles
and the sky lurching among
the leaves, the shape of it tilting
at me crushed under the sun.

The Old Pond, Ah!

What is Zen? *I do not understand.* What is Zen? *The silk fan gives me enough of a cooling breeze.* What is Zen? *Zen.*

1

Fleas, lice,
the horse pissing
near my pillow.

To be read with composure:
butterflies, my head
in a stream of champagne.

Basho comes
banging my bed
with his lantern,

I
who always sleep
on clean percale.

2

If you ask me
how are things?
And I answer

after the rain
the paths are dark
at the edges,

you might hit me
or twist my nose,

but I would not say
you are like a tiger.

3

One absolute emptiness, not
death, is there ever?

I do not know if the river
is fingers that flow in it
or channels the water cuts.

Neighbors

The light is thin,
slides into rooms in strips
filling the pillow creases of my skin;

there in a design
of windows red arms come,
and one hand travels up the glass with blinds.

We do not wholly
meet; blinking, we test
the whiteness of the day like moles.

Leopards swarm
over her walls and vines,
and fourteen minnows crawl across her lawn.

She may surprise
a peacock on my porch
or any wandering tail across the sky.

But she won't see
me back into my shadow
warm as hers. We'll share our ritual privately—

and light the gas,
and swing the faucets on,
and never speak about it when we pass.

Space

The shortest days of the year are long.
The shape of the world's the same, but we're not
used to it. This month again. We take off
our perfect heads as if to exchange them,
but they grow right back. The moon
like the crust of a great land turtle
rides by the window sliding its craters
past our eyes.

       Now we have found our real size
by that light, turn on the earth's own axis
where we've always turned, back to our dying,
back to our separate floating around the sun.

The other side of the moon's whatever they
tell us, owl-sockets, stale bread, having to call it
only what we know. If we could name it,
if we could take the light behind the surface
into our mouths.

       This month again.
Wet streets, glass wrinkled with rain,
the dark between us and the small
intricate clock still in its place. If we could
stop it, following trees in summer, to find
the child alive before the man, girl-child,
green lake giving back our image out of time.

When we are nowhere for each other's hands,
touching a face that isn't there, our fingers
end and we walk slowly out of the doorway wanting
and not wanting to go back. Something
that happens shows us who we are. The moon's dust.
How it comes down on us in columns
closing our eyes, whitening our shoulders
in the dark. It's the return that scares us.
And how we never seem to change.

December 1968

II

Is it not time that, in loving,
We freed ourselves from the loved one, and, quivering, endured:
as the arrow endures the string, to become, in the gathering
   out-leap,
something more than itself? For staying is nowhere.

Rainer Maria Rilke

It Stays

What fills this house,
slides under
the weather-stripping,
wagging branches
plugged with leaves
or buckled with fruit
will never be married.

If I grow friendly,
regard it calmly
as one strokes a child's
head talking to somebody
else, it leeches
in, breeding
its own disorder.

And if I lie down
under it, make
it as real as what
I have become,
it grows around me,
shoves its way
into my arms.

Jasmine, we shake
the air and vines
catch fire.
Flesh of the inner
flower, eyes
above me coming
through leaves.

The old nibble of lies
in the dark, vines
bursting fragrant
against my hair,
hurting my face.
They climb the walls
like toads, open

their tropical mouths
crowded with roots,
saying, you've got to
feed us, cracking
the paint, the plaster,
shaking me, nothing
I'll ever tame.

Some Credibles of Marriage

1

The man who counts his mules
and always has one missing
at last unmounts.
He sees the one he rides!
Ocarinas! Peacocks!
Then up again numbering
over and over,
it never comes out right.
Finally he walks to town.

2

The giants
we battle
come obstinate as ever.
Proceed like elephants
into the fierce country
of ruins.

3

To lose hate
is not to have love.
If we are
each his own Adam
avoiding,
under the branches
our conspicuous system of hideouts,
there is nothing much left
but a devotion of spinsters.

4

Though we deceive, and do
not navigate the things we say—
spiders, the instant
below the rolling wheel,
fingers, tongues,
mandolin, blather,
any—
people in love
keep talking.

5

More than the inch of feathers
on which the bird
depends,
the sea delivered
and the wings unbending
finding their shore,

dignity matters.
Is not a chance arrival
into the weather of flight.
Comes like a canopy
in the right season.

The Hunger Artist

"If I had found it, believe me, I should have made no fuss and stuffed myself like you or anyone else."

Franz Kafka

1

It's no use trying to find again
what it was like.
And the spectacle of it. The breasts
begin to go, skin
loosens under the chin.
You watch
an aging courtesan undress.

2

Him waiting, waiting as if
you never loved by night.
Long welts
of daylight, another bed.
To let it happen
easy as Eden, no wringing
of the mind, wrestle of leaves
to squeeze through.
His solemn arms, his room
not dark enough, your having
to be the way you are.
You fasten like things on a pond
to their own reflection.
Till he discovers that
you cannot play.

3

Remember your swimming
when a wave fell in.
Too stunned to fight the undertow,
you gave yourself up
dreaming to the pull.
When you lie down once more
in dangerous places
taking the fruit between your teeth,
there is always the light
thatched over another
who breathes beside you, entire,
strange to your wanting
even the least of what he was.

4

When plastic chairs in the kitchen
begin to crack, or fabric
on the footstool wears
through to the stuffing,
or the sink falls slowly down
from the level of the formica counter
because water got in
under the unseen wood and is secretly
chewing it all away;

when you look in the mirror
after everyone leaves in the morning,
and the only sound is the thin hum
of the furnace, and suddenly
it stops, and the house begins to tick,
and you see the small wrinkles

under your lashes smudged
with mascara you never get off,
and you make a terrible smile
watching them deepen and lengthen
like thin lines raked in the sand
of a perfect Japanese garden;

you feel everything
being eaten from its surface.
Soon there will be no covers
and what is under
will be exposed, wasted,
no longer able
to keep the flesh alive.

I Hear You

The promises of mother—
smiles, soft fingers
children could not touch.
You and your sisters
gliding like fish
(the tank was full
of your stare) to market
to market, sun
in your scarves, the ripple
of exquisite goiters.

You never wore a hat
except in mirrors,
your eyes were violet
under the veil,
under the knotted squares
calling me child.

But I went after you,
mother to mother,
put you together
when your bones rode you
apart. Something
was always breaking
down inside you.

Save me, you sob
in a dream, but nobody
runs like a friend
to your door. And I'm
in my own garden this time,
digging a ditch
for my heart.

What
did you give me, mother,
that you want it back?
An empty book to put
my poems in, peeled
apples, Patsy dolls.

Each day I sucked
at your virtuous breasts
and I'm punished
anyhow.

Mothers, Daughters

Through every night we hate,
preparing the next day's
war. She bangs the door.
Her face laps up my own
despair, the sour, brown eyes,
the heavy hair she won't
tie back. She's cruel,
as if my private meanness
found a way to punish us.

We gnaw at each other's
skulls. Give me what's mine.
I'd haul her back, choking
myself in her, herself
in me. There is a book
called *Poisons* on her shelf.
Her room stinks with incense,
animal turds, hamsters
she strokes like silk. They
exercise on the bathroom
floor, and two drop through
the furnace vent. The whole
house smells of the accident,
the hot skins, the small
flesh rotting. Six days
we turn the gas up then
to fry the dead. I'd fry
her head if I could until
she cried love, love me!

All she won't let me do.
Her stringy figure in
the windowed room shares
its thin bones with no one.
Only her shadow on the glass
waits like an older sister.
Now she stalks, leans forward,
concentrates merely on getting
from here to there. Her feet
are bare. I hear her breathe
where I can't get in. If I
break through to her, she will
drive nails into my tongue.

Always She Moves from Me

Always she moves from me,
climbs over the bridge, singing
with other swift daughters, leans
into shadows, calling her image
to rise from the water.

A flight in one direction,
where the long paths littered
with sun end, and the rocks
warm to the light, the alternate
touch of her running feet.

Wanting my self again, not lost
but at a distance, dark
among trees, I stumble uneven
ground. My shadow the color
of old leaves and slow

to find her, thick with my own
mother. If she could hear me
through the upstream air that hums
between us, I would repeat
my old articulate love,

but she hears only the plum tree
knock like a clapper in a gong
of blue, thighs deep in lilies,
and the branches closing
behind her where she goes.

Don't Look for Me, I'm Gone

Pawns taken, the red
queen cornered in the Grand
Tier, wearing her jewels
like skin, glitters.
They are figuring how
to finish her off. As if
the final move were theirs.

I've still got the paintings,
the daughters, a husband
and pots on the stove.
I'll lock the youngest
in a closet. She'll feed

on darkness, stay small
and white and difficult
to lose. One less
to listen to. All
talking at once—do this!
While I'm stroking my own
neck, flowing with pearls.

They marvel I manage,
as if who they're seeing
is there. Under the spangles
I'm breathing. Everyone
talks to my encrusted ear.

In Place Of Real Bulls

"We will render the offerings of our lips in place of real bullocks."
Hosea

In place of real bulls,
glistening flesh, surprises
lurching down the fields,
battering fences, scraping
their sides like barges,
let us give words.

Like a distribution of prizes
after the game. You'll squeeze them
cautiously out of your teeth,
lumpy with vowels.
I'll mutter you mushrooms,
elegant, undersized.

Notes from a Nine Room House

1

Ribs are important,
cheekbones, all that
hard structure under the flesh.
Don't tell me about
the human condition.
Even the postures
of love are absurd
if you see it that way.

Whatever we say
boils over.

If I smell so delicious,
why don't you take me to dinner
and eat me?

2

The wind comes in like a rock
the door you leave open.
Your mouth is filled with redemption.
What did you mean to bring?

You stop
for historical landmarks
as if they were real.

You will not see
from where you are
that the roses I arranged yesterday
are already dead.

3
I'm trying.
Nobody knows when I'm here
alone in the morning
drowning the cats.

I open my windows
wider than tracks,
arriving splendid
where I used to be.

But I still find
those long, white hands
in museums lifting
marigolds. The perfect
French gloves. Old
friends stroking themselves.

They walk in my garden
and never blink.
Their bodies surround me
like wickets. A fat
mallet keeps driving
me off the lawn.

4
No one
cuts fuchsias
for the house.

I manage
how they spill over the table,
needles of blood, tongues

from a lizard's mouth eating
their shadows off the wood.

They hang with the weight
of their own existence.
They are dying by water.

A contagion
of never waking.
Courtly, to drown
and barely lift an arm.

Her Going

As if I carried a charm
for daughters, I would carve a smile
each day and enter it, set it
between us like a pumpkin glowing.
Out of its hollow mouth,
the candle burned away.

No one will smooth her now
with promises. But when the sun comes
through the glass, I see her face,
smell the milky wrinkle of her skin,
feel the small shape of light
going out of my arms.

Eye

1

If she were Greek
she would have killed me,
axed the old mother
out of the play
         the way
a daughter's fury works.

I lie in my bandage of dark,
smelling orange and cabbage,
hearing the sounds of their seeing
TV the dishes the faucet everything
going ON.
         And the whole
unblocked field of their vision
hammers to get in my head.

2

Wheels of rain rock
through the streets.
They roll on the roof.
The sound of the water running
like teeth down the gutters.
Sons and their fathers.
              Daughters,
their mothers.

3

To be ice. To snap
brittle with cold.
To feel only this tightening
death under glass—how it fights
to get out!

　　　　Just a moth.
Crush its soft wings
till they sift in the palm
to fine powder.
　　　　　　Then small
household pets. The cat
in its elegant sleep, warming
the mohair blanket.
　　　　　　　Squeeze
its fine head in your hands,
hear the bones
　　　　　　crack
like fried fat.

At last your arm plunging
down through their flesh.
Slash at the children for laughing.
Rip the veins out of his neck.
Spit at them blind blind blind.

　　4
Oh loveless woman! Oh woman hauling huge sacks
of love you can't open! Oh woman whose lovers
bring plastic carnations! Whose husband says stop
the Chinese! Woman in smooth sheets holding
jars of dried roses! Who listens to Coltrane
in a gondola! Oh whore when the young move in!

Oh woman whose beauty was tulips, who sang
in your skin whether or not they were waiting!
Whose skin grows coarse under lotions! Whose
children are leaving and leaving! Who lies
in your own dark lacquer, dying behind your eyes!

Oh Rilke's girl at the window alone! And you
pouring tea at your table, the guests bumping
elbows and talking! And you in your milky
bath with aphorisms and bowls of daisies!
Buying tickets, fingering velvet, filling bags
in the supermarket. Alone. On the eighteenth
floor of the bank building and at sunrise
and in the dentist's chair. Alone.

5

And when the rage comes
         from a hive of hornets
walls of the house
         swell thick and hot

when the rage comes
         like the dead who aren't buried
doors won't open
         and the rooms stink

it has no way
         as water has of going
on down rivers
         to the impassive sea

when the rage comes
        she heaves an unripe apple
hard in my eye
        to make me know

how the heart
        sticks out like a toe
through a worn sock

and how it stays there
        staring
through the live hole

44

III

You never know what is enough unless you know what is more than enough.

William Blake

Foucault Pendulum

It is nothing we feel
    where our shoes
    stay still
    as they are

    where we lean
over pegs
        to the bronze ball
swaying
        its highlights
over the pit
        where the earth
rotates calm
        as a saucer
and the swing
        goes wider
than any
        small swing
    of our heads.

It moves
    though the shift
    of the ball never changes
    except in the eye.

It is not to be measured
    the world creaking slowly
    the tilt of a landscape
    the falling of things.

It's the floor
        that keeps turning
    outside of the mind

the pull of the tides
           oncoming of seasons
    your breath
    moving
    into my skin.

Lately

I am not prepared yet for the sacrifice
and what could I bring?
The sea is the color of unripe plums,
and waves lift out of it like altars.

I let cold splinters of water spill
through my hands while the sun goes
down behind the body of the world.
It doesn't get worse or better.

My hands grow whiter under the surf.
I see them give up their fingernails,
slowly the knuckles. And my rings float off.
It is painless. There is nothing to hold.

I believe what I feel. Great ice caps
melt at the poles. The oceans rise.
And I watch how the sand begins
to crumble wherever I stand.

For a Cold Night

1

Roof over roof, the darkness—
colder than clay.

The size of your back
covers the shape
of the moon.
                    We pull in
the chains of our eyes.

2

Pale juice of remembered berries.
The lake is around me,
undazzled.

                    If being loved
were all the heart requires . . .

I swim in it, gathering water
into my dwindling arms.

3

A tree climbs in through my window
louder than bells.
The tips of branches
start to ring.

Exile of indoor plants,
guppies in bowls.
                    The flytrap
masticates its bugs.

I pace the small floor of my head,
listening, listening.

Room

"O this is the creature that does not exist."
Rilke

1

The sky can't get in.
Or sun where you enter
the core of the wood.
Extravagant, burned-out
trees. There is no
provision for darkness.
Shadows flow smooth
down your skin, and the skin
of the tree thickens.
You stretch to his face,
and the flesh of your ribs
grows into his arms.
You give whatever is
possible. After so many
forests. And you are
slowly what you are
in any light.
               It happens
only when you give it
room. That milky beast.
Fed on the chance
that it might be,
it is. Destructible
as anything that lasts.

2

Lights hum at the window
like hives opened out.
They swarm through your head.

They move in the dark
of his fingers finding
your breasts.
               And laurel.
Changed back to woman,
more lavish than she
ever was. Who is he
sliding in your arms? What
will become of you?

  3
Is it because he
told you what he dreamed?
Drawing a boat through
the fountain. Carefully.
Fontainebleau's opulent
gardens. Or does it
grow to more than you
can manage as a game?
Every chateau in France.
Your belly is warm
and feathered. His mouth
is tasting your shoulder.
And the duck goes after
her babies in the pond.
Waking and waking and
waking, you breathe
the light from his skin.
A swimmer whose arms lift
heavy, suddenly.

4

You are behind the surface
of yourselves. His hand
strokes the outside
of your hand. Your colder
skin. Why does it
cry each time
at the tense bone until
the flesh gives in?
The sun is over
the great park. He has
gone out of you.

Poems for the End of the World

1

Just to the edge of the fog.
But we sailed into it,
there was no edge
that we could touch.
Till it was there
behind us, everywhere,
and we in the center
of a small clear space,
sails coming out of it
open
and the great grey side
of a ship.

2

We live
by extremities.
Even
the ends of fingers
hunger
for sons.

3

Now they hoist their heads
like flags.
They tie white scarves
over their eyebrows.
A sign
in the empty cities
everyone mourns.

Each day
they dust off the table
in Paris,
straighten
the chairs.

4

The unconditional harpy
waits among mirrors
tossing out wishbones,
cleaning her stationary ears.
Lights switch on and off
behind her tongue.
Sometimes a voice
that says a coin's two-sided
or that a bullet
travels seven years
to reach the sun.

5

"I dreamed of four cedars,
four sycamores, a hide
stuffed with straw
and an ox riding on them."

"The four cedars are four bedposts,
the four sycamores are four legs
of the bed, the hide stuffed with straw
is the mattress on which you sleep.

You will climb into bed
and never get out."

6

We sat in our rooms
like rabbits
and called them functional.

No one reached from his window
as far as his arms could stretch
to scrape the mortar,
wreck the bricks
of his apartment house.

No one painted
everything pink or yellow,
sawed up the walls,
filled up his rooms
with mud.

7

There was never enough
time to exceed
the flesh, to know
that borrowed rooms
unbalanced us as if
invisible owners tilted
the floor.

                Never
enough time to consider
the ends we had to outlive.

The skin still
rings like alarms.

8

I'm through, I am starting
to say when
the whole world comes
rolling over the slope
and the wheels still turning.

The earth doesn't rotate.
It wobbles. Everyone
grabs kids, pillows,
check books, collapsible
hatchets.

                   As if
we had some place
to go.

There She Goes

"And the earth will slip from under one and one shall fall with one's eyes on heaven."

Pascal

There she goes, falling
to the soft light that reddens hills and walls,
    all sides that shelter.
Even the four dark sparrows on her roof's
    peak shift the sky
rosy among them, push off into it
    like larger cinders.

She listens for the music
she has lost, rolls over warmer air,
    flapping her skin past
windows wide to heaven. Never looks down
    to see the earth turned
skyward, wrinkled, staggering with fire,
    to find familiar trees

some branch to hide in
and the leaves still cool above the burning
    where she touched and gave.
Not there, but up, up through the glittering
    algae of the night, up
with the other believers. Never discovers
    the available rocks.

Rites

I was the chosen,
coming too soon to the high station,
    bracelets of lilies,
        the green plume tall.

And time ran out in rivers.
I reached through windows
    after trees,
saw them away to darkness.
Slopes far ahead
    swam past in flower,
birds came upon me
    and were gone.

They severed the plume,
with it, the hair-lock
    down to the root.
Finally the head.
And into their vats
    the warm blood.

How does the festival
    of my becoming
smell in the meadow?
And who will have me?
No access to the ear of Princes,
    citizen,
    undeceived,
    but dead.

Rebecca

It's the duplicity that sticks—
that I would trick my husband when
he couldn't see. Rocking, he hugged
his knees and heard the meat already
ticking in its grease.
                                    Oh
we were quick about it then,
though Jacob was slow to move.
He used to squat all day in the tent,
feeding the fire with me. I watched
the blood run when he stripped the goats,
and helped him carry the skins behind
the trees. I wound the pelts around
his wrists, his smooth girl's neck,
and dressed him in his brother's clothes,
smelling of woods and wind, the wild
grass after a rain.
                                    I plotted
merely for a gift. Like any
clever woman at her stew. A pot
of deer, salt and fresh herbs.
It wasn't easy pacing inside my flesh
while Isaac ate, sucking my breath
between the cracks of my small teeth,
hotness climbing over my face, the way
I waited for him as a bride.
I listened still to water at the well,
my arm uplifted to the jug.

Clumsy at noontime in his night,
he wiped his mouth and shook the light
outside him, touching the wrong one.
His fingers, delicate as leaves,
dropped in the false skin.

Let people serve and nations bow
to thee.
And all the rest. It stays
in my ear like cramps. Blessed, blessed.

Holding On

Arms in the small
light   trying to hold
on to the skin
of our separate dark
the curtains move
the long night
covers us like wool

still we unroll
our separate comforts
over the single
bed   I close my eyes
to discover we pull
at each other's mouths
and what we listen for

comes only dumb
lips moving   silence
of whales   some
huge and hazardous
flesh   the walls
are leaving even
before they fall

Next Year, in Jerusalem

One by one, the ancient
shapes are dying.
But an old aunt leans there
from *seder* to *seder*
with her cancerous skin
flaking off the sides
of her nose.

Jerusalem waits
where it always was.
They are growing
deaf, though in different degrees.
Thin, yellow fingers twist
at their breasts
for the hearing-aid dials.
Should I repeat it
again for you? Slowly.

Turn up the sound. I am learning
their smiles. I am pleading.
Elijah's cup is untouched.
I hear myself hearing
my breathing. Loud.

How to Wait

I smooth the sheets. Lakes
in the snow. Rain forests.
Cities in caves. All
my inventions grow
beyond my willing them,
some place to go
when you are telling me
how to wait.

It's not too late.
The buffalo boy dreams
of riding lightly
in his whole skin. The girls
still move rivers
with their hands. Nothing is
less than what it seems.

But the children are old
repeating the names
of their fathers.
I make this bed
for us to sleep.

Above Vitebsk

The old man sitting on the roof
is really there. In fact,
he is an uncle.
And if the wagon gets up
off the road, it's only
one leap to roll sideways
over the town.

Such leaning and loving
high in the night sky,
who will come down?
Peddlers, sweethearts,
milkmaids with faces floating
or three-breasted dancers?

Your father in his herring shop
may have seen his fish
climb ladders, but you
conform to your own miracles,
flutter your own air.

The poet finds his head turned
upside down. The weightless
angel is in the child.
The child has wings.
The fiddle is musician,
plays itself.
What is earthbound?
Which of us must fall?

Pruning

I discovered them all at once filled
with leaves—but it was more gradual; ponds
dwindling underneath the wind until
all the water seemed to be gone.
    The greenness spilled out of my hands,
    and I forgot the way the spring began.

The weather turns to pruning, and I climb
from myself, up this rocking ladder
into the roses. (Will there be time
enough to burn the wreck I gather?)
    I hang my long arms in the air
    and lean against whatever's leaning there.

They yield themselves, brittle; no blooms
break low over the sour paths,
no opening fever, no fragrance bruised
in light. I make of them an ample death—
    as if I wished it final. But the stiff
    wood stays, cut only to the second leaf.

And a slow dark, sleep and a cold
ground will bring the small buds again
like sudden stings. The stalks grow old
as habit, luminous in the rain.
    Softly I move over the wet grass,
    stepping aside to let my footprints pass.

I learn my own renewal now:
root, stem, leaf, thorn, flower—
my wakenings, my sleep—warn how
the heart regresses quietly each hour
  to its center and the same heart leads
  to sunlight out of its own need.

IV

. . . we always set out to return
to solitude, a fistful of earth, to the empty hands.
George Seferis

Keep Moving

1

Thirty-five thousand feet
over the next place, Haydn
in my ears, you
in your separate flight.
                    A bright
cell humming through huge
pale country. Sun sliding
slowly off the wing.
                 Keep moving,
keep shipping out of ourselves.
Any sky to be lost in.

2

Push up these stairs
slivering white, blue
dolphins over the door,
hot wind on my skin like a plaster,
caught between walls and ruins
of walls.
             How do I climb
into the lives of strangers
or set my pulse by their time?

3

It goes on turning in my head
like an old reel. Moon-change,
tide-change, farther than ever
from the place you are.

Wave of the pulling gulls,
of the body's long shining,
of lively skin after love.
Wave of the light more real
than what it touches.

Wave against wave when the light
slips under, myself filling the dark
that no one fills.

####### 4
Each end of the line we wait
to go back, pass the last station
anxious at night. Some wooden
engine in us won't get off.
As long as the wheels creak
we are safe.
          But we move
through the gates like abandoned
children, wanting to be found.

####### 5
I'm sick of this traveling. The heavy
baggage of the flesh.
            And when
I pull the drapes, your face leaks
in. As when the shore swims
into focus through a field
of glass.

Here are the fish at Bergen
bunched in tin tubs. Their crazy
leaping out of the water as if
to be chosen. Dumb. Beat in the eyes
with a mallet.

When are we going home?

New Graveyard: Jerusalem

The earth runs furrows under my skin.
Landscapes arrange themselves
like pages turning, old brown
snapshots between my fingers,
patriarchs staining my thumbs.

I fit into their sky. I wrap their sun
around my arm. And I deceive them
looking for larger prophets.

I should make more of it, led here
by signs I always knew. Sometimes
I lick a stamp so long it doesn't stick.
Even the old extravagance of faith
forgets what it has to do.

                              I walk
the paths till they become huge
freeways that the dead ride on.
And I'm not sure who sleep away
their lives, what we are here for,
where they've gone.

Looking For Maimonides: Tiberias

Here is the place.
The flies are too fat
to rise from the dirt.
Three men in dusty caftans
come running with candles.
Their nails are the yellow
of their beards, greased
with doing the grieving.

The edge of his mind
was clean, with thirteen
signals staking out the way.
The whole of that warm ark
rocking order and light.

Whoever whitewashed the tomb
this year knocked over the can;
white islands puddle the ground.

I look away from them,
and the sun eats at my eyes.

There is a smell of rotting
melons where a grey cat stares.
Some sticky coins
compose their prayers.

He is not there.

Meron

"First is the fire that receives fire . . . the second . . . is the inmost fire which is joyful at the presence of the other . . . then comes the third fire which surrounds that brightness, wherein resides the terror. . . ."

Rabbi Simeon ben Yochai
The Zohar

1
This is the mountain
where ben Yochai walked.
I watch the mist move
up the sides like breath
into frozen air.
                    Earth
without form, no visible
light until the
                    Word.

Twenty-two letters join,
fly round, fling crowns
in every corner
of the unborn world.

The center
              bursts out
like a tree
              singing
the Holy Name.

I climb the stones and pull
the letters down on me.
They leap in my mind
like souls out of his
seven eyes.

Faces
I might have known,
paler than frost,
                    and one
who opens over the crest
her inmost fire. No longer
strange as the language
she could not pronounce.

Grandmother,
                    always pressing
money into my hand,
coin against coin,
gummy with candies
from her apron pocket.

    2
She showed me her real hair
once under the *sheytl*,
so withered thin
that it was almost gone
from being hidden.

No man could listen to her sing
or study near her dangerous arms
when she was beautiful, before
she shrank each year lower
and lower around her hips.

I wondered how she wore
my grandfather like a wig
at night over her small
white shape, gave him twelve
babies that she didn't want

and walked through Russian
winters in her sleep, running
down empty streets
to pound on shuttered
windows, bolted doors.

The Cossacks always
rode inside her head.

3
None of them came for me.
I cannot dream about
Theresienstadt.
                    Leave them
alone, unburied, leave them
forever in their open
ditch or floating heavy
in the smoke-sour sky.
See how they flourish
                    and multiply.

And if I stand here now
where every rock's a marker
for their unmarked graves, touch
these cold stones, the surface,
hardness of stone, not to be
touching who they were,
the skinny bones,
heaping small mountains
as a child builds blocks
counting as high as he can go,
six million bodies,
no one sees.

The Word
troubles another air. What
can the living cry for
to the dead?

4

At Meron I look down
into nothing. The sky is huge
with its own color, and the last
shapes of mist ease
to the sea.
            Nothing
will follow but the mist
again, over and over,
breath of their mouths.

Grandmother, more precious
as you grow more useless,
you are rocking into
His name.
            The letters rock
from ben Yochai's eyes.
The world is already made.

They knew the old words,
and they sipped the wine,
bunched between miracles
and fear.

            What corner
of the field is safe?
Why did you hide your hair?

The Western Wall

"What are they doing here? And why are they crying?"
Elie Wiesel

And so through the Jaffa Gate, the street
named David swaying with donkeys,
down the Street of the Chain, barrels
of spices and of fresh baked bread,
women with tin trays on their heads
and shapes of children running everywhere.

Down the old city—to the wall.
I stop and stare. The wall is thick
with its own silence. The men become
their fathers. Women cover up their arms,
their hair. And I am old with them
and they have held my children
with their dead.

          I move across the whole
world to the wall and with my fingers
touch against their touch the shadows
growing out of it like vines. The stone
is cold. As if my hand lies buried
under ground, it sucks the cold,
my palm is filled with it.

             And prayers.
The yellow papers in the wall, higher
than arms can reach. They fall
from every hollow, every crack,
fall in the small pores of my skin,
and I am huge with prayers I cannot hold.

Heavy with messages, I stay
until the wall goes out
beyond the wall, circles the Temple
and the Ark, the ruins below the paving
where we crowd, rocking with faces,
kings and priests, their eyes like animals
at night shining so fiercely through the dark
they pass between us and the wall,
and we become their shadows breathing
dust, breathing the place where we have been,
all that is written in the awkward flesh,
how the whole alphabet of yearning
makes no words, the unformed words
keep crying in our throats.

V

But paradise is barren and the angel stands in back of us; we must make the journey around the world and see if perhaps it is somehow open to us from the rear.

Heinrich Von Kleist

To Masaccio
(Seeing his "La Cacciata Dal Paradiso")

                    You painted
them as though you too were dispossessed.
You must have seen that place, ringing with birds,
stems growing and sunlight shaking the leaves.
You had to see it once the way it was.
Until, unsure of His own faithfulness,
He began to test the only faithful.

And where it ended, you began. For them.
I watch that naked man become himself,
and Eve, all bone again, woman and pain,
move slowly, human, into their private fear.
Out of the landscape of her mouth I hear
the cry, more terrible than any, being first.
She can't forgive her breasts. He hides his eyes
as a child, blindfolded in a game, still
hides from invisible angels, flaming swords.

Here on a wall in Florence, Maso, dead
at twenty-six, you knew what they knew:
the shape of every wilderness, so many
gardens gone, the animals all named,
the gates guarded. Each of us asking
where is there left to go?

Watts

For Sabatino (Sam) Rodia, builder of the Towers, who died in Martinez, California, July 16, 1965, before the riots.

1

My friend who married the girl I
introduced him to after he felt
my breasts under the steering wheel
of his parents' borrowed DeSoto,
and swims in a big jar
in the San Fernando Valley,

my friend who plucks tonsils
with manicured tweezers, and gave me
a Barlach woodcut of two agonized
women for my last birthday,
                              tells me
he's learning to shoot
with his children, teaching them how
with a gun, and last week
he hit the bull's eye at fifty feet
twenty times out of twenty.

The son who sings in the choir
wins prizes. The youngest, a girl,
plays the flute and the cello.
The middle one studies hard.

    Why?
I ask
wanting to start over.
    Why?

We all need a gun
in the house. Learn
to use one. The first time
I fired it, they jumped.
Now they love it. And Watts,
he says.
Think about Watts.

2

Monday morning and the red garbage
truck shifts up the hill, jerking
like bones, like California
sliding in the sea.
                    Bent,
with the big can full to his shoulder,
cigar in his teeth, tattoo on his arm,
and two flat boxes of slimy lettuce,
chicken bones, sardine cans,
used-up carbons stuck to his hands,
he climbs the path to the street
and heaves the dreck in.
                    What
do we keep?

3

I went to Watts to see
the Towers. To see the sky
come at me
in thin frames, bleached
by the bluer glass.

The Towers.
Flying like ladders, testing
a coolness that we never
reach.
                As if I raised
myself into that breach, as if
I climbed on coiled springs
                                into air.
(Taylor over the keyboard
                                lifting
the sound so fast his hands
are spaces that the wind
pours through.)

                        Broken mirrors,
and my face in parts,
the shapes of corn ears,
baskets, one thin shoe.

Thirty-three years, Rodia,
card number 6719 in the International
Hod Carriers, Building and Common
Laborers' Union, his single
trowel slapping the wet cement,
bending the hoops to let
the light come in, lifting
the junk, the junk
                        to spires!

The way trees grow and slowly,
ring over ring.

                    Plates,
abalone shells, bottles,
lengths of pipe.

                    Against
his death.

    4
Guns in warm houses,
rifles. Knives.

                    Glass
in the streets and burned-out
doors.

            I'm saving
finger nails, cut-off hair,
nothing that sticks or stays
the same, but still
it's there. Shape of my lap
turned into something different
when I stand.

            It grows.
Dead leaves and babies,
cancelled maps,
                    even
my shadows, reflections in water,
the loose skin over each
knuckle of my hand.

Mycenae, the Graves, the Gates

They are deep.
And we come all this way
to look down where
the treasure is gone.

It's always the last time.
I am smoothing a thin gold
mask to your face
as weightless as faith
in my hands.

We climb,
and the dry grass shakes
in the wind. It is burning
the edge of the graves.

The room is already old.
Mounds of soft earth
swell slowly. You
are making me
disappear.

Stone gates,
tense lions, the white sun
stopped in my groin. I am thinking
of when to be born.

The Turning

I can't remember how we got
to Spain. The dream
where we visit your place.
A path thick with dust
up the mountain. The higher

levels of the sun. This
is your hacienda. It is dry
and brown, grown over
with weeds and wilting vegetables,
the ground cracked.

There was a woman, of course,
instructed to grow orange trees
and lemon, date palms
and even bananas. Not
beans for her own kitchen.

Across the horizon,
in long black coats,
come the tall daughters,
cool faced,
with eyes of silver.

Each one wrapped tight
against her bones as if
the moon might enter her.
They are pale with craving
and nothing to feed on.

Why won't you complain
to the woman in charge?
She has killed what you came for.
Get rid of her.
All those dark ladies.

You turn away then, and I
follow you on the steep path.
The way down is the same
way. Only it's easier
once you leave.

Birds

Often I lose myself where no birds are:
no panic of wings,
no flapping on an open wind,
flight of no flight
unless my own,
unhinged.

I remember those silly pigeons
in Venice, plucking corn
out of my children's hair.
It was April. Sunlight
toppled over the Grand Canal.

I run, I run,
these moving parts all knee and ankle,
that meadow visible only
because I have not reached it yet
(I always leave the moment I arrive).

But I have seen them
coming toward me lightly
like a constellation of rain,
the soft sides pulsing.
Seasons when they hang
in a composition, fixed,
and up and down are weightless
and the same.

All that I am is all
I have not been allowed to be.
Is it those bodies
that I never touch?
Each of them quick
around me, wing-wide. Even
the brittle ones, most trivial
robins, small brown females
on my steps. Or sparrows,
beaks like bent thorns
nibbling the cool, uneven ground.
The compact fierceness
at the mouths of crows.

Let me come into them,
the air be full of
green on gold on purple
iridescence circling
the throats of doves.

Search

Well I ride down some endlessly
    feathered fins where the light can't follow,
      navigate by fever or by hinge.

A shadowy crab clicks
    under water stirring the sand,
      its gritty comfort, and I know

she's there in my own gills
    somewhere, eyes wide as nasturtiums,
      breast stroking out of the dark.

All Day   All Night   New York

1

In the middle of a cultivated
lake I wake up
on the second floor
of the Museum of Modern Art
surrounded by water-light
flowing through flowers
strokes of light
blue   green   rose
they tremble against my eyes.

2

Gulls hang tight
in their own wings.
Over the rail cold
runs in my face like tears
where one girl poet rode
back and forth
all night on the ferry
past the great lady
with her green spiked hair.

3

The trees are bare.
They are serious and moral
like worn-out lovers.
There's a hospital with fake
Greek columns where we wait.
Classic as minor
temples. Light drains
off them. The bus
is late.

4

Look how
that iron branch
bends to the sky, springs
with small lights,
flies out to Brooklyn
between two spires!
And as we cross
the red sun
gives off sparks.

5

The skin of your throat
is paler than mine.
All night they breathe, those
frail blue flowers, promising
only what we reach for.
Handles of light,
our wrists through water.
Silk I step out of
green   rose.

Aquarium

Fish under water, weaving the clear
and equal cubes with silent movement,
fins and eyes, leave no paths
as they pass. They are contained
in paleness like an inner rind,
and lose their shadows in a rain
of light through scales, transparent tails.

And we so late emerged (fin
that stretched to water pulled like a wing
to sky), see how the crabs step sideways
on the points of their slippery joints;
how catfish float, testing with short picks
of whiskers the liquid space before;
how fastening in fear, the sea
anemones close petal tentacles.

Like fugitive swimmers out of a dream
of tanks we come, compassless. Only
the small, round openings of our mouths
for signals. The shape of our softness public,
but secretly at home in warm waters.

Giant turtles just below the surface
hang from their own reflections, heavy
with overlapping plates of shell.
Light flows. We feel our way. Slowly
begin to close the bony pieces
of our disconnected selves.

PITT POETRY SERIES

COLOPHON

The poems in this volume are set in Baskerville, a type first used in the eighteenth-century. The Linotype cutting used here is most faithful to the original version, being produced from a complete font cast from the original matrices found at Paris in 1929.

The printing is directly from the type by Heritage Printers, Inc. The paper is Warren's Olde Style antique wove, and the cloth is by Columbia Mills. The design is by Gary Gore.